WILD CHIMPS
LIKE TO GET
DRUNK ON
FERMENTED
PALM SAP.

SNOW LEOPARDS
CAN'T ROAR.

IGUANAS CAN USE THEIR EYES TO COMMUNICATE.
IGUANAS LIKE IT HOT AND STICKY.

BEAGLES ARE AN OLD DOG BREED, SO OLD THAT THEIR EXACT BEGINNINGS ARE UNKNOWN.

THE FRENCH BULLDOG BREED ACTUALLY ORIGINATED IN ENGLAND.

THERE ARE
MORE THAN
FIFTY
DIFFERENT
KINDS OF
KANGAROOS.

KILLER WHALES (ORCAS) ARE NOT WHALES AT ALL, THEY ARE A SPECIES OF DOLPHIN.

LADYBUGS ARE ACTUALLY BEETLES. IN EUROPE THEY ARE CALLED LADYBIRD BEETLES.

ONE OF THE WAYS LLAMAS COMMUNICATE IS BY HUMMING.

Panda's have to
eat 25 to 90
pounds of bamboo
every day to meet
their energy needs.

POLAR BEARS ARE
STRONG SWIMMERS.

DOLPHINS USE TOXIC PUFFERFISH TO 'GET HIGH'.

GUINEA PIGS ARE
NEITHER PIGS
NOR FROM GUINEA.

KOALAS ARE NOCTURNAL
AND SPEND MOST OF THEIR
TIME ASLEEP IN TREES.

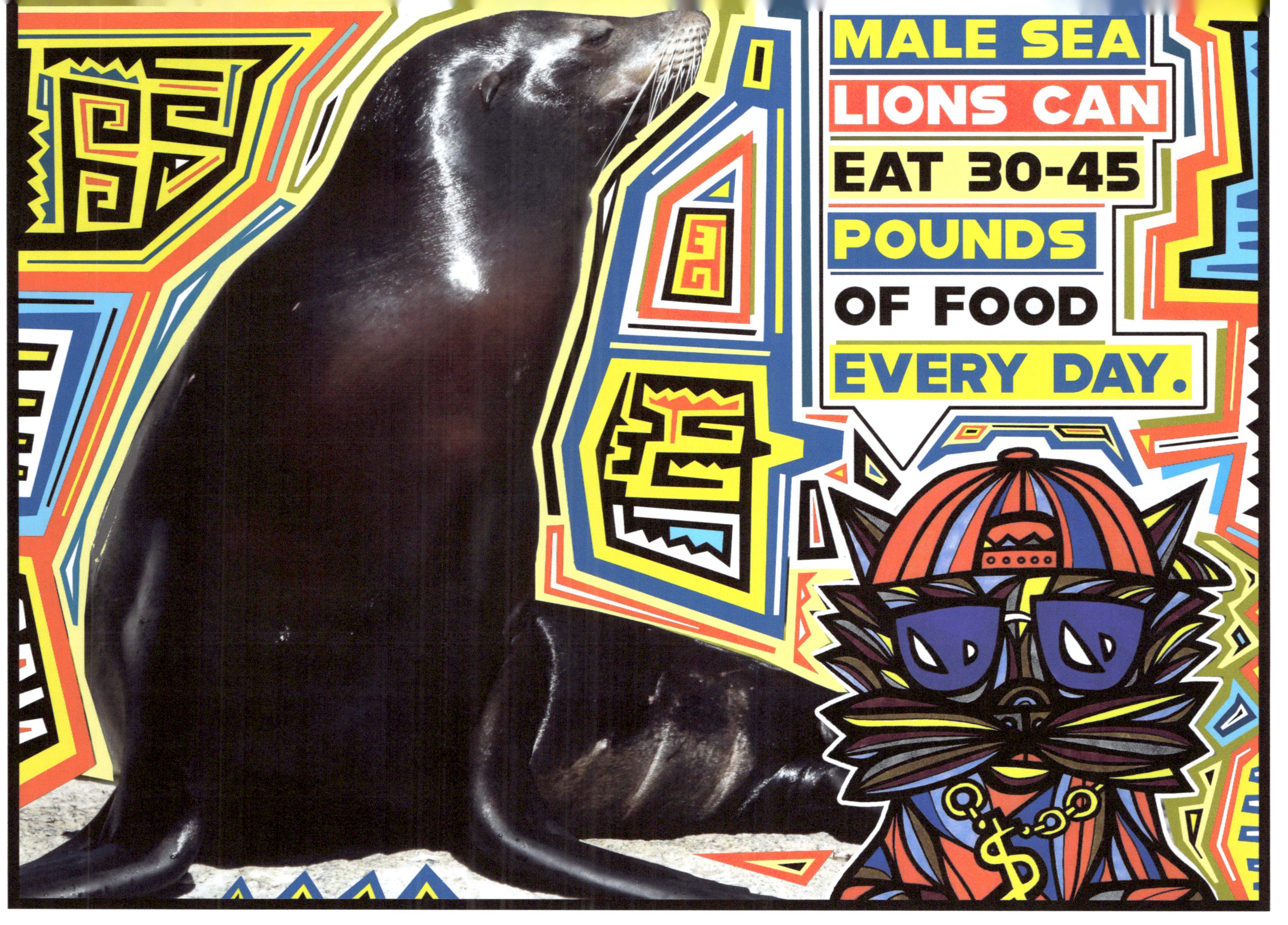
MALE SEA LIONS CAN EAT 30-45 POUNDS OF FOOD EVERY DAY.

LEOPARDS' EARS CAN HEAR FIVE TIMES MORE SOUNDS THAT THE HUMAN EAR.

HEDGEHOGS WILL EAT ONE-THIRD OF THEIR BODY WEIGHT IN ONE NIGHT.

FERRETS SLEEP FOR
20 HOURS PER DAY.

THE NAME "JAGUAR" COMES FROM A NATIVE AMERICAN WORD MEANING "HE WHO KILLS WITH ONE LEAP".

MEERKATS
BABYSIT EACH
OTHER'S PUPS.

THANK YOU.
THE END.

COPYRIGHT 2020
BY EDDIE ALFARO
ALL RIGHTS RESERVED.

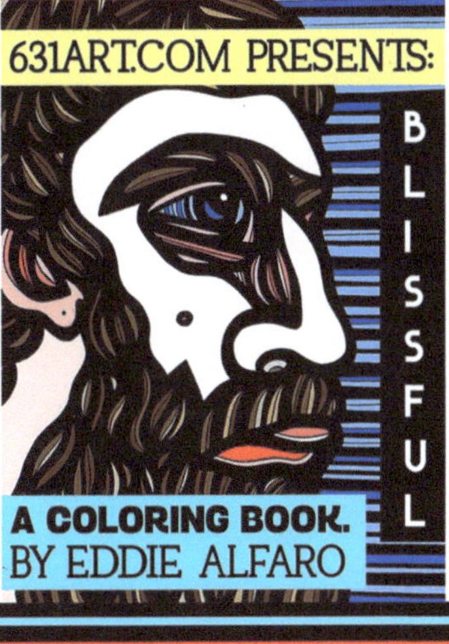

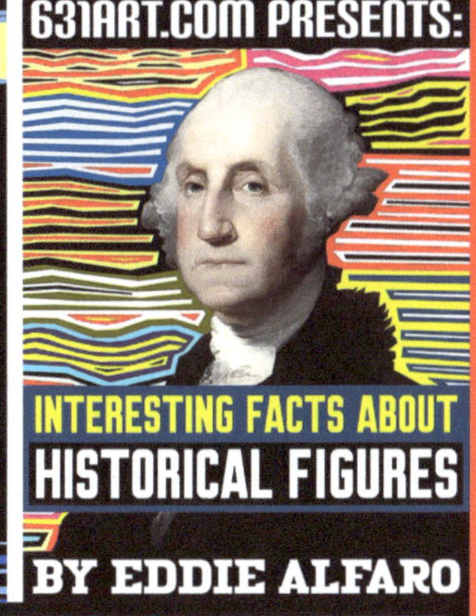

MORE BOOKS AT:

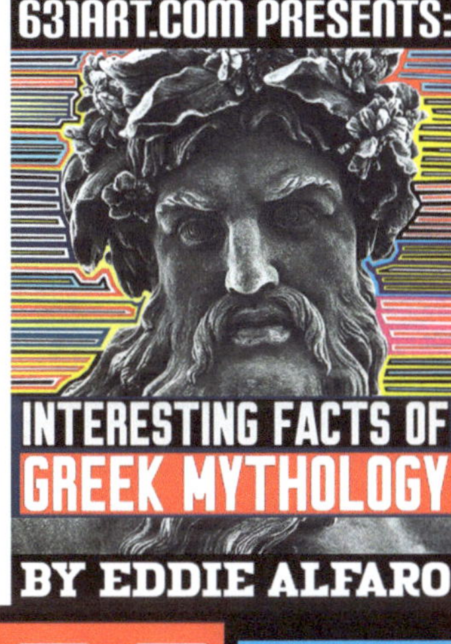

631ART.COM

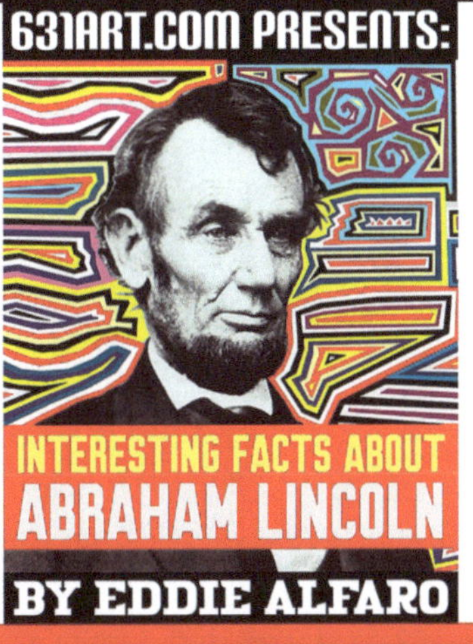